MOTIVATIONAL

AND

INSPIRATIONAL

QUOTES

JUSTIN J. KOJOK

JUSTIN K. KOJOK

Printed Worldwide

First Printing 2025

First Edition 2025

ISBN: 978-1-966348-07-8 (Paperback)

ISBN: 978-1-966348-06-1 (eBook)

10 9 8 7 6 5 4 3 2 1

Contact: author@kojokbooks.com

Website: https://kojokbooks.com

DISCLAIMER NOTICE:

Please note the information contained within this book is for educational purposes only. All effort has been made to present accurate, up to date, and reliable, complete information.

By reading this book, the reader agrees that under no circumstances is the author responsible for any losses, direct or indirect, which are incurred because of the use of information contained within this book, including, but not limited to, errors, omissions or inaccuracies.

DEDICATION

To my late Mother, Mary Konjit Kojok,

And to all widows, whether departed or alive.

Your courage to hold on to life after losing your husbands to death is a testament to resilience and love. You are the silent warriors, the unwavering pillars, and the unsung heroines whose strength lights the way for others.

For the nights you endured without answers, the days you faced with bravery, and the hope you continue to nurture. May these words honor your journey, inspire your spirit, and remind you of the immeasurable impact of your love and perseverance.

BOOKS BY JUSTIN K. KOJOK

1. Driving For Justice
2. Intercessor: *A Collection Of My Fervent Prayers*
3. Whispers in the Vineyard
4. Cybersecurity: Safeguarding Our Digital World

Please scan this QR code to buy these books.

TABLE OF CONTENTS

.

INTRODUCTION

In a world of perpetual motion, where challenges outnumber successes, and uncertainty obscures clarity, we crave a beacon to guide us through the maze of life. Motivational and inspirational quotes serve as beacons for the heart and mind, providing wisdom, hope, and strength in the form of deeply meaningful words. This book is more than a collection of quotes; it is a journey. It invites you to explore the realms of courage, resilience, dreams, connections, and progress—to unlock the power within yourself and see the extraordinary in the ordinary. Each part is carefully crafted to speak to your soul, addressing themes that touch every corner of human existence. From finding your purpose to building lasting relationships, embracing change, and leaving a legacy, this book provides the keys to igniting transformation.

The most significant challenges of life often require not just action but inspiration, effort, and empowerment. The quotes in these pages are meant to uplift, challenge, and remind you of the immense potential within. They are drawn from the universal truths of human experience, designed to transcend cultures and time, speaking directly to what makes us resilient, hopeful, and uniquely powerful.

As you turn these pages, let the words settle into your heart. Reflect on their meaning, apply their wisdom, and let them guide you toward clarity, strength, and purpose. You can revisit this book repeatedly, each time discovering a fresh perspective, a renewed sense of purpose, or the courage to take the next step.

Motivational and Inspirational Quotes are divided into ten parts, each focusing on a vital aspect of life—from courage and resilience to innovation and progress. Each section offers carefully written, original quotes to motivate, inspire, and empower you. The intention is simple yet profound: to remind you that you are not alone, that greatness lies within you, and that an opportunity to rise comes with every challenge.

This is your time to reconnect with the essence of who you are and what you can achieve. Take these words as your fuel, your compass, and your encouragement. Whether you're seeking a spark of hope, a push toward your goals, or a moment of peace, let this book be a companion for your journey.

- PART I -

Courage, Resilience, and Inner Strength

Though they test us in ways we never would have thought possible, every difficulty offers a chance to uncover latent stores of bravery, fortitude, and inner strength. This section of the book honors the relentless spirit that, in the face of tremendous circumstances, refuses to give up. Every quotation in this part is meant to spark the fire inside you so that you may stand tall in the storm, climb back after every fall, and gracefully and deliberately negotiate the complexity of life. These remarks should serve as a reminder that bravery is the decision to go despite fear, not the absence of it. Your capacity to adapt, persevere, and flourish— that which is resilience— is inside you.

COURAGE

1. "Courage isn't the absence of fear; it's the triumph over it."

2. "Every brave step forward is a rebellion against doubt."

3. "True courage is speaking your truth, even when your voice shakes."

4. "It takes more courage to grow than to remain where you are."

5. "Courage is the spark that ignites the fire of possibility."

6. "Dare to stand alone; sometimes courage is a solitary act."

7. "The bravest hearts are those that beat for others."

8. "Courage transforms ordinary lives into extraordinary stories."

9. "The greatest acts of courage are those unseen by the world."

10. "Courage is not what you have—it's what you choose to become."

11. "The foundation of courage is rooted in belief, not certainty."

12. "Boldness is the gateway to the life you've dreamed of."

13. "Courage isn't born; it's sculpted by the challenges we face."

14. "Fear tests us, but courage defines us."

15. "A single act of courage can echo through eternity."

16. "The risk of courage is outweighed by the reward of growth."

17. "Courage is the antidote to regret."

18. "Sometimes, courage means simply putting one foot in front of the other."

19. "Heroes are made in moments of quiet courage."

20. "Courage isn't flashy; it's persistent."

21. "To stand up for what's right is the truest form of bravery."

22. "In the face of doubt, courage is your unwavering shield."

23. "Courage doesn't promise safety; it promises growth."

24. "The measure of courage is found in the size of the challenge."

25. "You don't need to roar to be courageous—sometimes a whisper is enough."

26. "The first step in courage is believing that you're capable."

27. "Courage begins where comfort ends."

28. "Facing fear is a declaration of self-trust."

29. "Courage bridges the gap between who you are and who you can be."

30. "In the battlefield of life, courage is your strongest weapon."

31. "Fear sets the stage; courage steals the spotlight."

32. "Courage shines brightest when the darkness feels absolute."

33. "Every act of courage writes a new chapter of resilience."

34. "The path of courage is paved with the stones of self-doubt."

35. "Courage whispers, '*Try again,*' when failure shouts, '*Stop.*'"

RESILIENCE

1. "Resilience is not bouncing back; it's leaping forward."

2. "Every scar is a testament to a battle won by resilience."

3. "Resilience whispers, '*You can,*' even when the world says, '*You can't.*'"

4. "The strongest steel is forged in the hottest fire."

5. "Resilience grows when you refuse to let setbacks define you."

6. "To bend without breaking is the art of resilience."

7. "Resilience turns adversity into the canvas for your masterpiece."

8. "A resilient spirit is the armor that shields against despair."

9. "Fall seven times, rise eight—resilience is the refusal to quit."

10. "Resilience is the silent strength that rebuilds after the storm."

11. "Resilience is the bridge between struggle and triumph."

12. "Challenges test our limits; resilience proves them wrong."

13. "A resilient mind is a fortress that even doubt cannot breach."

14. "The beauty of resilience is found in its quiet persistence."

15. "Adversity is the soil in which resilience takes root."

16. "Resilience transforms pain into purpose."

17. "What breaks some strengthens others—resilience makes the difference."

18. "Every setback is an invitation to resilience."

19. "A resilient heart knows that storms don't last forever."

20. "Resilience doesn't erase pain; it redefines it."

21. "The power of resilience is revealed in moments of weakness."

22. "Resilience doesn't mean unbroken; it means unstoppable."

23. "Like water through stone, resilience shapes its own path."

24. "Resilience is the courage to hope when hope feels lost."

25. "In the ashes of failure, resilience builds anew."

26. "A resilient soul carries the lessons of yesterday with the hope of tomorrow."

27. "Resilience finds a way when the path disappears."

28. "It's not the fall that defines you, but the rise."

29. "Resilience is the art of holding on while letting go."

30. "The stronger the storm, the deeper resilience digs."

31. "Resilience doesn't wait for the world to be fair."

32. "When life whispers '*give up*,' resilience screams '*keep going*.'"

33. "Resilience is the quiet resistance to life's chaos."

34. "The foundation of resilience is built with moments of surrender and strength."

35. "Every small triumph fuels the engine of resilience."

36. "Resilience isn't about perfection; it's about progress."

37. "The resilient see obstacles as opportunities in disguise."

38. "When hope flickers, resilience fans the flame."

39. "Resilience walks hand in hand with perseverance."

40. "The roots of resilience grow deeper with every challenge faced."

INNER STRENGTH

1. "Inner strength begins with the belief that you are enough."

2. "The quietest battles within often require the greatest strength."

3. "Inner strength is the compass that guides you through uncertainty."

4. "True power lies not in what you show but in what you endure."

5. "Inner strength grows in the shadows of self-discovery."

6. "What the world sees as calm is often the result of inner storms."

7. "The roots of inner strength are nourished by self-love."

8. "Inner strength is a whisper that says, '*Keep going.*'"

9. "Strength is not the absence of struggle but the mastery of it."

10. "Your inner strength is the foundation of unshakable confidence."

11. "Inner strength emerges when you learn to trust yourself."

12. "The greatest victories are often fought within."

13. "Inner strength is the lighthouse during life's darkest storms."

14. "What you survive shapes your inner strength."

15. "Inner strength is the quiet resolve to keep climbing."

16. "When the world is loud, inner strength listens within."

17. "True strength is holding on when every part of you wants to let go."

18. "Inner strength isn't found; it's built."

19. "Your greatest weapon is the strength you hold within."

20. "The journey inward is the path to strength."

21. "Inner strength grows stronger with every act of self-compassion."

22. "The foundation of strength is the acceptance of vulnerability."

23. "Inner strength transforms pain into wisdom."

24. "It's not the size of the challenge, but the depth of your strength."

25. "Strength whispers, '*You're enough,*' when doubt shouts, '*You're not.*'"

26. "Inner strength is the courage to sit with your fears."

27. "A strong spirit cannot be broken by temporary defeats."

28. "The weight of inner strength can move the mountains of doubt."

29. "Strength is being at peace with who you are."

30. "True strength knows when to rest and when to rise."

31. "Inner strength grows through the cracks of broken moments."

32. "What feeds your spirit fuels your strength."

33. "Inner strength is resilience rooted in self-belief."

34. "Strength doesn't mean you'll never fall—it means you'll always rise."

35. "When the winds of doubt howl, your inner strength stands firm."

- PART II -

Dreams, Aspirations, and Vision

Dreams are the seeds of possibility, and aspirations are the steps we take to bring them to life. Vision gives our efforts focus and direction, turning the intangible into reality. This part celebrates the power of dreaming big, setting ambitious goals, and pursuing them with unwavering determination.

Every quotation helps you to see the beauty in your dreams and the power of your ambitions. Vision helps you to glimpse the possibilities ahead, even if the road seems unknown. Let these words inspire your passion and serve as a reminder that one dream starts every big success.

DREAM DEVELOPMENT

1. "Dreams are the seeds of change; plant them with purpose."

2. "The size of your dream determines the scale of your journey."

3. "Dreams don't expire; they evolve as you grow."

4. "A dream without action is just a wish waiting for life."

5. "Great dreams are born in the quiet spaces of possibility."

6. "Dreams are whispers of the life you're meant to live."

7. "Your dreams are not random; they echo your potential."

8. "Every step you take toward a dream brings it closer to reality."

9. "Dreams fuel the fire of persistence when the world feels cold."

10. "To dream is to dare, and to dare is to live fully."

11. "Dreams are bridges from who you are to who you can be."

12. "Never apologize for dreaming too big—limits exist only in the mind."

13. "Dreams demand courage, but they repay with transformation."

14. "The most powerful dreams are those that scare you a little."

15. "A fulfilled dream is a gift you give your future self."

16. "Dreams are the blueprints; action is the architect."

17. "If you can dream it, you've already begun to create it."

18. "Dream boldly, but remember to act with steady hands."

19. "The weight of a dream is carried by a resilient heart."

20. "Dreams unfold in layers—peel back fear to reveal the truth."

21. "Don't fear dreaming; fear the life you'll live without it."

22. "Your dreams are your destiny, speaking in the language of hope."

23. "Even the smallest dreams hold the power to change your world."

24. "Dreams are the universe's way of showing you what's possible."

25. "When your dreams align with your purpose, magic happens."

26. "A dreamer's heart is their greatest treasure."

27. "Dreams create paths where none existed before."

28. "Dream with your eyes open, and you'll see the possibilities."

29. "The world belongs to those who believe in their dreams."

30. "Dreams are the colors that paint life's black-and-white moments."

31. "A dream pursued with passion becomes a calling."

32. "Your dream is the light that guides others out of darkness."

33. "Never underestimate the power of a dream's first spark."

34. "The beauty of a dream lies in its ability to inspire others."

35. "A life without dreams is like a sky without stars."

ASPIRATIONS

1. "Aspirations shape the direction of your life's journey."

2. "What you aspire to defines what you're willing to fight for."

3. "Aspirations give life its meaning; they're the compass of your soul."

4. "The height of your aspirations reflects the depth of your belief."

5. "Aspire not for perfection but for progress."

6. "Aspirations grow in the soil of self-belief."

7. "The best aspirations challenge you to exceed your limits."

8. "What you aspire to achieve shapes who you become."

9. "Aspirations are the roots of greatness; nurture them daily."

10. "Every aspiration begins with the decision to try."

11. "Your aspirations are mirrors reflecting your true potential."

12. "Let your aspirations inspire others to dream bigger."

13. "Aspire to create, not just to consume."

14. "An aspiration is a promise you make to your future self."

15. "The world changes when people aspire to make it better."

16. "Aspirations fuel the engine of ambition."

17. "Aspire to live a life that tells a meaningful story."

18. "Your aspirations are the stepping stones to your purpose."

19. "The fire of aspirations burns brighter when shared with others."

20. "Aspire to leave a legacy of love and impact."

21. "The strongest aspirations are those rooted in passion."

22. "Aspire to be a better you—not a perfect one."

23. "Your aspirations define the horizon you'll chase."

24. "Dreams inspire; aspirations act."

25. "Aspire to live boldly, not quietly."

26. "Aspirations are the wings that lift you above challenges."

27. "Aspire to contribute as much as you consume."

28. "Your aspirations light the path through uncertainty."

29. "An aspiration turns the ordinary into the extraordinary."

30. "Aspire to build, to grow, and to thrive."

31. "Let your aspirations be louder than your doubts."

32. "Aspirations are the heartbeat of progress."

33. "The weight of aspirations is balanced by the strength of action."

34. "Aspire to create ripples that reach far beyond yourself."

35. "In aspiring for more, you discover who you are meant to be."

VISION

1. "Vision is the art of seeing what is invisible to others."

2. "A clear vision brings clarity to life's chaos."

3. "Without vision, even the greatest potential remains dormant."

4. "A powerful vision transforms obstacles into stepping stones."

5. "Vision is the light that guides dreams into reality."

6. "The sharpest vision cuts through the fog of doubt."

7. "Your vision defines the legacy you leave behind."

8. "Vision begins where sight ends."

9. "A true vision is fueled by passion and driven by purpose."

10. "Your vision is the map, and your actions are the journey."

11. "Great visions inspire not just you but those who follow."

12. "A vision worth pursuing will demand your best self."

13. "Vision gives wings to dreams and direction to aspirations."

14. "The strongest vision withstands the weight of skepticism."

15. "Visionaries see beyond the present into the realm of possibility."

16. "Your vision is your superpower; use it wisely."

17. "A vision backed by determination becomes unstoppable."

18. "Vision is the heartbeat of leadership and innovation."

19. "The future belongs to those with the courage to envision it."

20. "Vision ignites change; it challenges the status quo."

21. "A shared vision creates a united purpose."

22. "Vision is the silent force behind every great achievement."

23. "Dare to dream, but more importantly, dare to envision."

24. "Visionaries don't follow paths—they carve them."

25. "Vision is the blueprint of your highest potential."

26. "A strong vision thrives even in the face of adversity."

27. "The clearest vision sees both the destination and the journey."

28. "A Vision fuel hope and builds resilience."

29. "Vision transforms a dream into a reality with impact."

30. "The world changes when enough people share a powerful vision."

31. "A vision is a promise made to the future."

32. "Your vision should scare you—it means you're dreaming big enough."

33. "Vision sees opportunity where others see limitation."

34. "A compelling vision attracts those who believe in the impossible."

35. "Vision connects your purpose to the needs of the world."

36. "The clarity of your vision defines the sharpness of your focus."

37. "Vision is the lighthouse guiding you through uncharted waters."

38. "Those with vision see potential where others see obstacles."

39. "A vision crafted with care is a life lived with intention."

40. "Your vision determines the life you're building, brick by brick."

- PART III -

Growth, Transformation, and Change

Growing is an ongoing process of becoming—of transforming into the person you are supposed to be. While change is the spark that starts the process, transformation is the link from where you are to where you hope to be. This part exhorts you to welcome change as an essential force for development, to consider transformation as a possibility for rebirth, and to embrace the potential of personal development. These quotations act as road guides, providing knowledge and inspiration to help you to keep ahead. Growing calls for bravery; transition calls for resilience; change honors those who welcome it with open arms.

PERSONAL GROWTH

1. "Growth begins where your comfort zone ends."

2. "Personal growth isn't a destination; it's a lifelong journey."

3. "True growth requires both patience and persistence."

4. "Every lesson learned is a step toward personal evolution."

5. "Growth thrives in the soil of self-reflection."

6. "To grow, you must let go of what holds you back."

7. "Growth is not about perfection but about progress."

8. "When you embrace challenges, you cultivate personal growth."

9. "Growth demands that you trade excuses for effort."

10. "Every day, you grow a little stronger, even if you don't see it."

11. "Growth transforms failure into a stepping stone."

12. "To grow, you must be willing to unlearn and relearn."

13. "The price of growth is discomfort; the reward is transformation."

14. "Your potential is limited only by your willingness to grow."

15. "Growth begins with the courage to face your fears."

16. "Change your thoughts, and you'll ignite your growth."

17. "Growth is a quiet revolution happening within you."

18. "The seeds of growth are watered by self-compassion."

19. "Every choice you make shapes the person you're becoming."

20. "Growth is the art of turning wounds into wisdom."

21. "Embrace growth and the world around you will evolve too."

22. "Growth requires looking inward before moving outward."

23. "Growth is not measured in leaps but in steady steps."

24. "The path to growth is paved with curiosity and courage."

25. "Growth teaches you to find strength in vulnerability."

26. "Your growth inspires others to seek their own."

27. "Growth begins when you decide to stop settling."

28. "To grow is to honor the person you're becoming."

29. "True growth comes from transforming pain into purpose."

30. "Growth is the bridge between who you are and who you can be."

31. "Let growth whisper in your ear: '*You're capable of more.*'"

32. "Growth doesn't happen by accident—it's a deliberate choice."

33. "Every experience, good or bad, holds the key to growth."

34. "Growth shines brightest in moments of perseverance."

35. "Your greatest investment is in your own growth."

TRANSFORMATION

1. "Transformation begins with a single brave decision to change."

2. "True transformation is born from discomfort and courage."

3. "Transformation isn't becoming someone else—it's becoming fully yourself."

4. "The butterfly was once a caterpillar that embraced change."

5. "Transformation is proof that growth is happening within."

6. "The most profound transformations happen in the quiet moments."

7. "Every transformation starts with the question: What's next?"

8. "To transform, you must first trust the process."

9. "Transformation requires releasing the old to embrace the new."

10. "A transformed life begins with a transformed mindset."

11. "Transformation is less about doing and more about being."

12. "Every storm carries the potential for transformation."

13. "Transformation begins when you stop running from who you are."

14. "You are one choice away from a completely different life."

15. "Transformation demands vulnerability, but it rewards with strength."

16. "The power of transformation lies in your ability to adapt."

17. "Transformation is the bridge between hope and reality."

18. "The first step to transformation is letting go of fear."

19. "Transformation doesn't happen overnight— it's a persistence process."

20. "Transformation begins where your excuses end."

21. "To transform your world, you must first transform your mind."

22. "Transformation is about progress, not perfection."

23. "A transformed life reflects the lessons learned in adversity."

24. "Transformation starts with believing that change is possible."

25. "The beauty of transformation is found in its unpredictability."

26. "Transformation asks: Are you willing to become more than you are?"

27. "In the fire of change, transformation forges a stronger you."

28. "Transformation demands that you trade certainty for possibility."

29. "Every small transformation leads to a bigger revelation."

30. "Transformation means embracing the unknown with open arms."

31. "Your transformation can light the way for others."

32. "Transformation turns doubt into determination."

33. "The scars of transformation tell the story of resilience."

34. "Transformation starts with a vision and grows with action."

35. "Transformation is the art of turning dreams into reality."

CHANGE

1. "Change is the wind that carries you to new horizons."

2. "Change doesn't wait for permission—it demands action."

3. "Every great journey begins with a single act of change."

4. "The pain of change is temporary; the reward is lasting."

5. "Change is the teacher; growth is the lesson."

6. "To change your life, you must first change your mindset."

7. "Change challenges you to step into the unknown and grow."

8. "Embrace change, for it's the only constant in life."

9. "Change is the catalyst for transformation and renewal."

10. "The power of change lies in your willingness to adapt."

11. "Change isn't easy, but it's always worth it."

12. "The beauty of change is that it creates endless possibilities."

13. "Change requires courage, but it rewards with progress."

14. "Don't fear change; fear staying the same."

15. "Change begins with a whisper of dissatisfaction."

16. "Change is proof that life is never stagnant."

17. "In every change lies an opportunity for growth."

18. "The heart of change beats in moments of decision."

19. "To embrace change is to honor life's natural rhythm."

20. "Change challenges you to become who you're meant to be."

21. "The first step toward change is letting go of resistance."

22. "Change reshapes the future in ways you can't yet imagine."

23. "The art of change is learning to flow with its currents."

24. "When change feels impossible, remember: You've done it before."

25. "Change pushes you out of comfort and into courage."

26. "Every ending is a change in disguise, leading to a new beginning."

27. "Change is a conversation between your fears and your dreams."

28. "To change is to grow; to resist is to stagnate."

29. "The power of change lies in its ability to redefine you."

30. "Change is a gift wrapped in the paper of uncertainty."

31. "Your life changes the moment you decide to act."

32. "Change doesn't mean forgetting; it means evolving."

33. "In the face of change, resilience becomes your anchor."

34. "Change rewrites the story of your life, one chapter at a time."

35. "To embrace change is to step into your next adventure."

36. "Change is the melody of life's most transformative songs."

37. "Every change is an invitation to discover something new."

38. "Change empowers you to create the life you desire."

39. "Change is the language of opportunity."

40. "The courage to change today shapes the world you'll see tomorrow."

- PART IV -

Kindness, Connection, and Relationships

Kindness is a universal language; connection is the lifeblood of human experience; and connections form the cornerstone of a meaningful existence. This section of the book looks at the transforming potential of kindness, the depth of connection, and the beauty of relationships that support and prolong our lives.

Every quotation reminds one of the values of empathy, compassion, and mutual respect. Whether you are strengthening current ties or creating new ones, let these words motivate you to lead with compassion, foster deep connections, and treasure the relationships that bring delight and direction into your life.

KINDNESS

1. "Kindness is a ripple that can create a tidal wave of change."

2. "A small act of kindness can transform a life."

3. "Kindness is a language that everyone understands."

4. "Be kind, for kindness costs nothing but means everything."

5. "True kindness shines brightest in moments of struggle."

6. "Kindness is the glue that holds humanity together."

7. "The simplest gestures of kindness often have the deepest impact."

8. "Kindness is giving without expecting anything in return."

9. "A single act of kindness can ignite hope in a weary heart."

10. "Kindness is contagious—spread it generously."

11. "In a world of noise, let kindness be your voice."

12. "Kindness is the bridge that connects strangers as friends."

13. "Kindness grows when it's shared without hesitation."

14. "Acts of kindness are the seeds of a better tomorrow."

15. "Kindness is the compass that guides us back to humanity."

16. "Even the smallest act of kindness can light up a dark world."

17. "Kindness is the armor that protects the soul from bitterness."

18. "Be kind—it's the greatest strength disguised as gentleness."

19. "Kindness doesn't need an audience; it needs a willing heart."

20. "True kindness is showing up for others when it's inconvenient."

21. "Let kindness be your legacy in a world hungry for love."

22. "A kind heart is a treasure the world can never lose."

23. "Kindness is the antidote to division and despair."

24. "In the presence of kindness, even the hardest hearts can soften."

25. "The gift of kindness is one size fits all."

26. "Kindness isn't an action; it's a way of being."

27. "Kindness is a superpower—use it every day."

28. "The beauty of kindness is that it multiplies as it's shared."

29. "Kindness is the thread that weaves compassion into action."

30. "Kindness has the power to heal wounds unseen."

31. "When in doubt, choose kindness—it's always the right answer."

32. "Kindness turns strangers into allies and enemies into friends."

33. "A kind word can open a door that's been closed for years."

34. "Kindness is the light that shines in the darkest corners."

35. "The true test of kindness is how you treat those who can give you nothing."

CONNECTION

1. "Connection is the invisible thread that ties us all together."

2. "True connection begins when you see the world through another's eyes."

3. "The strength of any bond lies in the depth of its connection."

4. "Connection doesn't require words; it requires understanding."

5. "We grow stronger when we lean into genuine connections."

6. "A meaningful connection can change the trajectory of a life."

7. "The power of connection is found in its authenticity."

8. "Connection is the heartbeat of human existence."

9. "In every connection lies an opportunity to learn and grow."

10. "The beauty of connection is its ability to transcend differences."

11. "Connection begins with listening, not just hearing."

12. "When you connect with others, you discover the best parts of yourself."

13. "True connection is built on trust, not perfection."

14. "Connection is the bridge between isolation and belonging."

15. "A strong connection is the foundation of a lasting relationship."

16. "The most profound connections often happen in the quietest moments."

17. "Connection requires vulnerability; it's the price of authenticity."

18. "When we connect, we create space for understanding and love."

19. "Genuine connection is a mirror reflecting mutual respect."

20. "Connection transforms strangers into friends and friends into family."

21. "A single connection can light up an entire network of hope."

22. "Connection is a two-way street paved with empathy and care."

23. "The threads of connection weave the fabric of community."

24. "Connection doesn't need proximity; it needs intention."

25. "The beauty of connection is that it grows with time and effort."

26. "In connecting with others, we find pieces of ourselves."

27. "Connection is the art of seeing beyond the surface."

28. "The soul craves connection; it's the essence of being human."

29. "To connect is to say, 'I see you, and you matter.'"

30. "Connection brings warmth to a world that can often feel cold."

31. "A shared laugh is one of the simplest forms of connection."

32. "True connection survives distance, time, and silence."

33. "In every handshake, there's potential for a deeper connection."

34. "Connection flourishes when nurtured with kindness and understanding."

35. "The power of connection lies in its ability to heal loneliness."

RELATIONSHIPS

1. "Relationships thrive on trust, grow with care, and endure with love."

2. "The heart of any relationship is built on understanding."

3. "Strong relationships are forged in the fires of shared experiences."

4. "Relationships aren't perfect; they reflect mutual effort."

5. "True relationships are grounded in respect, not convenience."

6. "The best relationships are those where both feel seen and valued."

7. "Relationships bloom where empathy and patience meet."

8. "A healthy relationship is a partnership, not a possession."

9. "Relationships flourish when both give without keeping score."

10. "The foundation of every great relationship is open communication."

11. "A relationship built on honesty is unshakable."

12. "The beauty of relationships lies in their ability to teach us love."

13. "Strong relationships weather storms because their roots run deep."

14. "Relationships are the mirrors that reflect our deepest truths."

15. "A meaningful relationship grows stronger through shared vulnerability."

16. "Every relationship is a lesson in love, trust, and forgiveness."

17. "The best relationships are those that celebrate individuality."

18. "A true relationship is built on mutual respect and shared dreams."

19. "In relationships, it's the little things that matter most."

20. "A relationship without trust is like a house without a foundation."

21. "Relationships heal when both choose understanding over judgment."

22. "To love in a relationship is to grow together through every season."

23. "The strength of a relationship is measured by its resilience in hard times."

24. "A loving relationship is a safe harbor in life's turbulent seas."

25. "Great relationships are about giving, not taking."

26. "The most valuable currency in a relationship is time spent together."

27. "Every relationship is an opportunity to give and receive love."

28. "Healthy relationships are built on balance, not control."

29. "True relationships are nurtured, not demanded."

30. "A relationship rooted in kindness will always find its way."

31. "The beauty of a relationship is its ability to grow with time."

32. "A relationship's strength lies in its ability to adapt and evolve."

33. "The heart of a relationship beats strongest in acts of love."

34. "A relationship that values laughter is the one that lasts."

35. "The best relationships create space for growth and individuality."

36. "Love is the soul of every meaningful relation-ship."

37. "Relationships aren't perfect, but they are perfectly worth it."

38. "In the garden of life, relationships are the most beautiful blooms."

39. "Relationships thrive on honesty, even when it's hard."

40. "The essence of every relationship is the con-nection of two hearts."

- PART V -

Self-worth, Confidence, and Empowerment

Your self-worth is your foundation, confidence is your strength, and empowerment is your ability to create change. This section is a celebration of your intrinsic value, encouraging you to embrace your uniqueness, believe in your abilities, and take control of your narrative. The quotes here are designed to uplift, inspire, and remind you that you are enough, just as you are. Empowerment begins with recognizing your own power and extends to inspiring others to do the same. Let these words serve as a daily affirmation of your worth and a call to action to live boldly and authentically.

SELF-WORTH

1. "Self-worth is not earned; it's inherent—claim it boldly."

2. "Your value isn't determined by others; it's defined by you."

3. "Recognizing your worth is the first step toward fulfillment."

4. "Self-worth grows when you stop seeking validation from others."

5. "You are enough, just as you are—never forget that."

6. "True self-worth isn't measured in achievements but in authenticity."

7. "Your worth doesn't decrease because of someone's inability to see it."

8. "The foundation of self-worth is built on self-respect."

9. "Celebrate who you are—your worth is undeniable."

10. "Self-worth is the anchor that holds you steady in storms."

11. "The moment you realize your worth, you stop settling for less."

12. "Self-worth is the quiet confidence that whispers, '*I deserve this.*'"

13. "Your worth is not tied to what you do but who you are."

14. "Honor your worth by walking away from what diminishes you."

15. "Self-worth means loving yourself even on the hard days."

16. "When you value yourself, the world learns to value you too."

17. "True self-worth is unshaken by the opinions of others."

18. "Your worth is infinite; never let anyone make you feel small."

19. "To know your worth is to unlock your true potential."

20. "Self-worth begins where comparison ends."

21. "You are worthy of love, success, and every good thing."

22. "Believing in your worth is the ultimate act of self-love."

23. "Your worth isn't negotiable—it's a fact."

24. "The journey to self-worth begins with accepting yourself."

25. "Self-worth isn't arrogance; it's self-respect in its purest form."

26. "You are your greatest asset—invest in your worth."

27. "The world sees you through the lens of your self-worth."

28. "Don't shrink to fit; your worth deserves space to shine."

29. "Your worth isn't earned through perfection but through authenticity."

30. "Self-worth means refusing to trade your dignity for approval."

31. "Every step you take toward self-love raises your sense of worth."

32. "Knowing your worth is the foundation of inner peace."

33. "Your worth doesn't lie in what you lack but in what you are."

34. "Self-worth is the compass that guides you toward fulfillment."

35. "A person who knows their worth becomes unstoppable."

CONFIDENCE

1. "Confidence is not about being perfect; it's about being authentic."

2. "The roots of confidence grow in the soil of self-belief."

3. "Confidence is quiet—insecurities are loud."

4. "True confidence is walking into the unknown with trust in yourself."

5. "Confidence isn't arrogance; it's self-assurance in action."

6. "When you believe in yourself, the world starts to believe in you."

7. "Confidence is built one small victory at a time."

8. "Your confidence is your superpower—use it wisely."

9. "Confidence grows when you stop fearing failure."

10. "To be confident is to know you're capable, no matter the outcome."

11. "Confidence isn't born; it's cultivated through effort and experience."

12. "True confidence is rooted in the acceptance of who you are."

13. "The more risks you take, the stronger your confidence becomes."

14. "Confidence is the bridge between hesitation and action."

15. "When you carry yourself with confidence, the world takes notice."

16. "Confidence is the courage to try, even when success isn't guaranteed."

17. "You don't need to be fearless to be confident; you just need to act."

18. "Confidence is the light that shines from within."

19. "The foundation of confidence is built on self-trust."

20. "When you trust your abilities, confidence follows naturally."

21. "Confidence isn't about never doubting; it's about doubting and doing it anyway."

22. "Stand tall, even when the world tries to make you small."

23. "Confidence grows when you choose progress over perfection."

24. "True confidence is knowing your worth without needing to prove it."

25. "Confidence is the voice that says, '*I can*,' when doubt whispers, '*You can't*.'"

26. "Your confidence inspires others to believe in themselves."

27. "Confidence is not a destination; it's a journey of self-discovery."

28. "To be confident is to embrace your uniqueness unapologetically."

29. "Confidence means trusting your instincts and following your heart."

30. "The beauty of confidence is that it empowers everyone around you."

31. "Confidence transforms fear into determination."

32. "Wear your confidence like armor—it protects and empowers."

33. "Confidence turns obstacles into opportunities for growth."

34. "When you show up with confidence, you open doors to possibility."

35. "True confidence radiates from self-awareness and self-acceptance."

EMPOWERMENT

1. "Empowerment begins with the conviction that you are capable."

2. "To empower yourself is to unlock your limitless potential."

3. "Empowerment is taking control of your story and rewriting the ending."

4. "True empowerment comes from within, not from others."

5. "Empowerment is the ability to create change in your own life."

6. "The first step to empowerment is believing in your own strength."

7. "Empower yourself, and you'll inspire others to do the same."

8. "Empowerment is the courage to speak up and be heard."

9. "True empowerment lifts others while elevating yourself."

10. "Empowerment is claiming the space you deserve without apology."

11. "The most powerful tool for empowerment is self-knowledge."

12. "Empowerment thrives when fear is replaced with determination."

13. "Empowered people empower others—be the ripple of change."

14. "To be empowered is to know you have the power to choose."

15. "Empowerment means owning your journey every step of the way."

16. "True empowerment is found in the freedom to be yourself."

17. "Empowerment grows when you turn obstacles into stepping stones."

18. "When you empower your mind, you empower your life."

19. "Empowerment isn't about control; it's about liberation."

20. "Empowerment is the strength to stand firm in your values."

21. "To empower is to turn potential into action."

22. "Empowerment is the art of turning dreams into reality."

23. "The empowered soul sees possibility where others see limits."

24. "Empowerment starts with a decision to take responsibility for your life."

25. "The empowered mind dares to think differently."

26. "Empowerment is rising after every fall, stronger than before."

27. "An empowered life is a life lived with purpose."

28. "Empowerment is the spark that ignites the fire of change."

29. "True empowerment is about progress, not perfection."

30. "Empower yourself by learning to say no to what doesn't serve you."

31. "Empowerment is creating opportunities where none existed before."

32. "To empower yourself is to become the hero of your story."

33. "Empowerment doesn't wait for permission—it takes action."

34. "The essence of empowerment is knowing you are enough."

35. "An empowered heart is one that loves without fear."

36. "Empowerment is standing tall, even when the odds are against you."

37. "When you empower your voice, you empower your soul."

38. "True empowerment is building bridges, not walls."

39. "Empowerment turns hope into action and dreams into reality."

40. "Empowerment isn't a gift you receive; it's a strength you claim."

- PART VI -

Action, Achievement, and Success

S uccess begins with action. This part of the book focuses on turning intentions into achievements and dreams into reality. Action is the driving force behind progress, and achievement is the result of consistent effort and determination.

Each quote is a call to take that first step, to keep moving forward, and to celebrate every milestone along the way. Success is about reaching the destination and growing through the journey. These words will motivate you to take charge of your goals, stay focused on your vision, and embrace the satisfaction of hard-earned success.

ACTION

1. "Action is the spark that sets your dreams ablaze."

2. "The future belongs to those who act in the present."

3. "Small actions, when consistent, create monumental change."

4. "An idea without action is like a bird without wings."

5. "Action is the antidote to fear and hesitation."

6. "Your dreams are waiting on the other side of action."

7. "Success begins the moment you take the first step."

8. "Action transforms intention into reality."

9. "Every small step forward is progress in disguise."

10. "Don't wait for the perfect moment—create it through action."

11. "Courage fuels action, and action fuels change."

12. "Action requires no permission; only a decision."

13. "Your actions today shape the life you'll live tomorrow."

14. "Action is the bridge between goals and accomplishments."

15. "Action isn't always loud; sometimes, it's quiet perseverance."

16. "The greatest plans mean nothing without action to back them."

17. "To act is to honor the power of now."

18. "Action transforms hope into tangible results."

19. "Your actions define your character more than your intentions."

20. "Bold action is the language of ambition."

21. "Procrastination steals dreams; action restores them."

22. "The first step is always the hardest but also the most important."

23. "Action doesn't guarantee success, but inaction guarantees failure."

24. "Every action is a vote for the person you wish to become."

25. "Action requires you to step out of your comfort zone."

26. "Each action you take sends a message to your future self."

27. "The secret to achieving big things is taking small, consistent actions."

28. "Your actions are the truest reflections of your priorities."

29. "To act is to show faith in your own potential."

30. "Action is where courage and determination collide."

31. "In the rhythm of life, action is the beat that drives progress."

32. "Dreams demand action to become more than fleeting thoughts."

33. "Action speaks the loudest when words fall short."

34. "In every step forward, action turns possibility into reality."

35. "When you take action, you give your dreams permission to grow."

ACHIEVEMENT

1. "Achievement is the reward for persistent effort and unwavering belief."

2. "Each achievement, no matter how small, builds momentum for the next."

3. "Achievement is less about luck and more about preparation meeting opportunity."

4. "Celebrate your achievements—they are the milestones of progress."

5. "Achievement begins with a vision and grows with determination."

6. "Every achievement is a reflection of the challenges you've overcome."

7. "Achievement is proof that you're capable of more than you imagined."

8. "To achieve is to turn effort into excellence."

9. "The road to achievement is paved with resilience and grit."

10. "Achievement isn't about perfection; it's about progress."

11. "Big achievements are the sum of small, consistent victories."

12. "Achievement is the art of turning ambition into reality."

13. "Your greatest achievements often arise from your greatest struggles."

14. "Achievement isn't a destination—it's a series of stepping stones."

15. "With each achievement, you redefine what's possible."

16. "Achievements inspire confidence and fuel future ambitions."

17. "The beauty of achievement lies in the journey it requires."

18. "Achievement is a measure of your courage to take risks."

19. "True achievement uplifts not just yourself but those around you."

20. "To achieve is to believe in the power of persistence."

21. "Every achievement begins with the decision to try."

22. "Achievement grows in the fertile soil of discipline and focus."

23. "The sweetest achievements are those born of hard work and dedication."

24. "Achievement is not accidental; it's intentional effort realized."

25. "Celebrate your achievements, but never stop striving for more."

26. "Achievement transforms dreams into milestones of success."

27. "Behind every achievement is a story of determination."

28. "Achievements are the footprints of a life well-lived."

29. "The best achievements are those that align with your purpose."

30. "Achievement requires effort, but its rewards last a lifetime."

31. "Every achievement is a testament to your resilience and growth."

32. "Achievements remind us that persistence is always worth it."

33. "To achieve greatness, you must first believe it's possible."

34. "Achievement requires focus, determination, and a willingness to grow."

35. "Your achievements are proof that you're capable of the extraordinary."

SUCCESS

1. "Success is the byproduct of passion, purpose, and perseverance."

2. "True success is measured in joy, not just accolades."

3. "Success begins with believing that you are worthy of it."

4. "The path to success is rarely straight but always worth it."

5. "Success is built on the foundation of consistency and effort."

6. "To succeed is to honor your potential with action."

7. "Success is less about speed and more about direction."

8. "The secret to success lies in mastering the art of persistence."

9. "True success uplifts others as it elevates yourself."

10. "Success isn't just achieving goals; it's growing through the process."

11. "Celebrate every small success—it's a step toward your bigger dreams."

12. "Success is a habit built on daily effort and intention."

13. "Define your own success, or the world will do it for you."

14. "Success requires both ambition and action in equal measure."

15. "A successful life is one lived with purpose and passion."

16. "Success isn't about avoiding failure; it's about learning from it."

17. "The greatest successes are born from the greatest challenges."

18. "True success feels like alignment, not just accomplishment."

19. "Success grows when you nurture your talents with effort."

20. "Your success is a reflection of your courage to keep going."

21. "Success is the harmony of hard work and unwavering belief."

22. "To succeed is to inspire others to see what's possible."

23. "Success doesn't come from luck; it comes from preparation."

24. "Success demands that you outwork your doubts and fears."

25. "The definition of success is living a life you're proud of."

26. "True success is giving your best effort every single day."

27. "Success is the culmination of choices made with intention."

28. "Real success leaves a legacy that inspires future generations."

29. "Success is a journey, not a finish line."

30. "A successful person is one who stays true to their values."

31. "The key to success is starting before you're ready."

32. "Success isn't found in shortcuts but in the lessons along the way."

33. "True success means balancing ambition with gratitude."

34. "Success isn't just reaching the top; it's lifting others as you climb."

35. "The sweetest successes come after the hardest struggles."

36. "Success isn't about being the best; it's about doing your best."

37. "The path to success is walked by those who never give up."

38. "Success is found in the details of dedication and effort."

39. "True success honors the journey as much as the destination."

40. "Success is living a life that aligns with your deepest values."

- PART VII -

Hope, Faith, and Positivity

Hope is the light that guides us through the darkness; faith is the trust that keeps us going, and positivity is the way we view obstacles as chances rather than as problems. This part honors the tenacity of the human spirit, the strength of belief, and the continuing force of optimism.

Every quotation reminds you to keep hope, trust in the road, and approach life with a good attitude since it provides an inspiring and motivating message. Allow these words to provide solace and a reminder that, even under the harshest of circumstances, better days are ahead.

HOPE

1. "Hope is the light that shines even in the darkest nights."

2. "When everything feels lost, hope whispers, '*Try one more time.*'"

3. "Hope is the bridge that connects dreams to reality."

4. "Every sunrise is a reminder that hope renews itself daily."

5. "Hope isn't passive; it's the active choice to believe in better."

6. "In the soil of adversity, hope plants seeds of possibility."

7. "Hope fuels the heart when the road feels endless."

8. "Hope doesn't demand certainty; it asks for courage."

9. "Even the smallest spark of hope can ignite great change."

10. "Hope is the anchor that keeps us steady in life's storms."

11. "Let hope guide you when the path is unclear."

12. "Hope grows when nurtured with resilience and faith."

13. "Hope isn't about ignoring pain; it's about trusting that healing will come."

14. "In every ending, hope sees the potential for a new beginning."

15. "Hope is the quiet voice that says, '*You'll get through this.*'"

16. "Carry hope in your heart, and you'll never walk alone."

17. "Hope transforms obstacles into opportunities for growth."

18. "When the world says '*no,*' hope whispers '*yes.*'"

19. "Hope thrives in the belief that tomorrow holds possibilities."

20. "Hope isn't just a feeling; it's a choice to move forward."

21. "Hope gives wings to dreams and strength to actions."

22. "With hope, even the impossible becomes a challenge worth pursuing."

23. "Hope doesn't erase struggle, but it makes survival meaningful."

24. "In the silence of uncertainty, hope hums a steady tune."

25. "Hope is the first step on the road to triumph."

26. "A hopeful heart sees rainbows amid storms."

27. "Hope is the architect of brighter days."

28. "Where hope exists, possibilities are endless."

29. "Hope is the glue that binds broken dreams."

30. "The essence of hope is found in its persistence."

31. "Hope doesn't wait for conditions to be perfect; it thrives in the imperfect."

32. "Every act of hope is a declaration of resilience."

33. "Hope is a magnet that pulls us toward possibility."

34. "Hope is the foundation on which courage stands."

35. "Never underestimate the strength that hope can bring to a weary soul."

FAITH

1. "Faith is trusting the unseen with unwavering belief."

2. "Faith is the courage to move forward without guarantees."

3. "In the absence of answers, faith steps in to guide."

4. "Faith doesn't eliminate fear; it empowers you to face it."

5. "Faith is the bridge between doubt and certainty."

6. "A life of faith is a life lived with purpose and trust."

7. "Faith is knowing the sun will rise, even when the night is long."

8. "True faith grows stronger in the face of adversity."

9. "Faith fuels the soul when logic falls short."

10. "Faith isn't about perfection; it's about persistence."

11. "Faith sees the potential where others see only obstacles."

12. "The strength of your faith determines the resilience of your spirit."

13. "Faith is the compass that points toward your true north."

14. "Faith doesn't promise ease; it promises peace in the journey."

15. "To walk by faith is to confidently embrace uncertainties of life'."

16. "Faith whispers, '*You are not alone,*' in life's quietest moments."

17. "Faith doesn't demand proof; it thrives on trust."

18. "True faith doesn't falter in the face of failure."

19. "Faith is the seed from which courage grows."

20. "Faith empowers you to take the leap, even when you can't see the landing."

21. "When all else wavers, faith remains steady."

22. "Faith turns doubt into determination."

23. "The beauty of faith lies in its simplicity and strength."

24. "Faith lights the way when the path is hidden."

25. "Faith isn't passive—it's the active choice to trust and move forward."

26. "Faith sees potential in every challenge and opportunity in every trial."

27. "A heart filled with faith knows no limits."

28. "Faith gives meaning to the chaos and hope to the uncertainty."

29. "Faith reminds us that every ending holds the seed of a beginning."

30. "Faith isn't about knowing what's next; it's about trusting you'll get there."

31. "True faith grows in the soil of patience and perseverance."

32. "Faith transforms the impossible into the inevitable."

33. "When you walk by faith, every step becomes a victory."

34. "Faith is the anchor that keeps you steady in life's storms."

35. "To live in faith is to live in harmony with hope and trust."

POSITIVITY

1. "Positivity is the lens that transforms obstacles into opportunities."

2. "A positive mindset creates a positive life."

3. "Even in the darkest moments, positivity finds the light."

4. "Positivity isn't about ignoring struggles; it's about facing them with strength."

5. "A positive thought can change the direction of your day."

6. "Positivity turns challenges into stepping stones for growth."

7. "The ripple effect of positivity can change the world."

8. "Positivity is a habit that begins with gratitude."

9. "A positive heart is the most powerful tool you possess."

10. "In every difficulty, positivity uncovers hidden blessings."

11. "The energy of positivity attracts possibilities."

12. "Choose positivity—it's a decision that transforms outcomes."

13. "Positivity thrives in the presence of hope and faith."

14. "Even the smallest dose of positivity can uplift a weary spirit."

15. "Positivity doesn't deny reality; it enhances your approach to it."

16. "When you focus on the good, the good gets better."

17. "Positivity is contagious—spread it freely."

18. "A positive attitude turns hard times into valuable lessons."

19. "Positivity fuels resilience and ignites change."

20. "Look for the silver lining; positivity will help you find it."

21. "Your mind is your garden—positivity plants the seeds of growth."

22. "Positivity is the silent strength behind every great achievement."

23. "The more you cultivate positivity, the brighter your life becomes."

24. "Positivity doesn't erase pain; it gives you the strength to endure it."

25. "A positive outlook invites opportunity into your life."

26. "Positivity is the gift you give yourself and others."

27. "Each moment holds the potential for positivity to bloom."

28. "Positivity sees possibilities where others see dead ends."

29. "Positivity is the thread that weaves happiness into your days."

30. "A positive mindset turns limitations into stepping stones."

31. "Positivity creates space for solutions to emerge."

32. "Your greatest power is the ability to choose positivity every day."

33. "Positivity is a decision that leads to transformation."

34. "Optimism is the heartbeat of positivity."

35. "With positivity, every challenge becomes a stepping stone."

36. "Positivity breathes life into your dreams and courage into your actions."

37. "A positive spirit inspires others to rise above challenges."

38. "Positivity is the light that shines through every storm."

39. "Choose positivity—it will always choose you back."

40. "Positivity transforms the ordinary into the extraordinary."

- PART VIII -

Wisdom, Knowledge, and Understanding

Knowledge applied is wisdom; understanding is the link between us and more fundamental truths.

This part of the book is devoted to developing insight, supporting curiosity, and motivating the search for information.

The quotations here challenge readers to consider, advance knowledge, and stress the need to know others and ourselves. Experience shapes wisdom; knowledge broadens through curiosity; understanding deepens the ties binding us together.

Allow these words to lead you toward more clarity, closer relationships, and a more rich viewpoint of life.

WISDOM

1. "Wisdom is not in knowing everything but in understanding enough."

2. "True wisdom lies in listening more than speaking."

3. "Wisdom turns mistakes into stepping stones for growth."

4. "The journey to wisdom begins with curiosity."

5. "A wise person learns even from their enemies."

6. "Wisdom is seeing beyond the moment to understand the whole story."

7. "To be wise is to know when to act and when to wait."

8. "Wisdom is the art of turning knowledge into action."

9. "A wise heart values kindness over being right."

10. "Wisdom doesn't shout; it whispers through experience."

11. "Patience is the companion of wisdom."

12. "Wisdom grows in the soil of reflection and humility."

13. "A wise person knows the power of a well-placed pause."

14. "Wisdom is learning from the past while building for the future."

15. "The seed of wisdom is planted in the field of mistakes."

16. "True wisdom understands that not every battle is worth fighting."

17. "The wiser you become, the less you need to prove."

18. "Wisdom sees possibilities where others see limitations."

19. "Wisdom is understanding that the journey is just as important as the destination."

20. "A wise mind is open to new perspectives."

21. "Wisdom grows when we embrace uncertainty with courage."

22. "True wisdom honors the lessons life has to offer."

23. "Wisdom teaches us that silence can speak volumes."

24. "A wise soul finds clarity in the midst of chaos."

25. "Wisdom understands that strength lies in restraint."

26. "Wisdom is the ability to navigate complexity with simplicity."

27. "True wisdom inspires others to think deeply and act kindly."

28. "Wisdom grows in the space between experience and understanding."

29. "A wise person values questions more than answers."

30. "Wisdom is knowing that growth often requires letting go."

31. "True wisdom balances the head and the heart."

32. "The path to wisdom is paved with humility."

33. "Wisdom doesn't age; it deepens with time."

34. "True wisdom seeks understanding, not dominance."

35. "A wise person builds bridges, not walls."

KNOWLEDGE

1. "Knowledge is the key that unlocks endless possibilities."

2. "The pursuit of knowledge ignites the fire of self-discovery."

3. "True knowledge empowers you to make better choices."

4. "Knowledge grows when shared with an open heart."

5. "Learning is the ladder that takes you to new heights of knowledge."

6. "Knowledge is the foundation on which innovation is built."

7. "A curious mind is the gateway to unlimited knowledge."

8. "Knowledge is not just power; it's the freedom to explore and grow."

9. "The more you know, the more you realize how much you have yet to learn."

10. "Knowledge is the seed; understanding is the harvest."

11. "True knowledge bridges gaps and fosters connection."

12. "The search for knowledge is a journey without end."

13. "Knowledge without application is like a map never used."

14. "To learn is to grow; to grow is to live fully."

15. "Knowledge expands when you seek to understand, not just to know."

16. "A mind that seeks knowledge never stagnates."

17. "The beauty of knowledge lies in its ability to inspire."

18. "Knowledge isn't found in answers, but in the questions, you dare to ask."

19. "Each book read is a doorway to new knowledge."

20. "True knowledge is built on the courage to challenge assumptions."

21. "Knowledge sharpens the mind and nourishes the soul."

22. "The pursuit of knowledge is the pursuit of freedom."

23. "Every lesson learned adds to the treasure chest of knowledge."

24. "True knowledge humbles you, even as it empowers you."

25. "Knowledge is the light that dispels the shadows of ignorance."

26. "The mind grows richer with every ounce of knowledge it absorbs."

27. "Knowledge transforms lives when paired with action."

28. "A knowledgeable mind sees beyond appearances to understand truth."

29. "Knowledge is the compass that guides you toward your purpose."

30. "The thirst for knowledge fuels a life of endless discovery."

31. "True knowledge isn't static; it evolves with experience."

32. "Knowledge equips you to navigate the unknown with confidence."

33. "The roots of knowledge are watered by curiosity."

34. "Knowledge connects the dots of life's bigger picture."

35. "Seek knowledge not for status, but for growth."

UNDERSTANDING

1. "Understanding begins where judgment ends."

2. "To understand is to see with both the mind and the heart."

3. "True understanding requires listening without the intent to reply."

4. "Understanding bridges the gap between differences."

5. "The foundation of understanding is built on empathy."

6. "To seek understanding is to value connection over division."

7. "Understanding transforms confusion into clarity."

8. "True understanding is born from genuine curiosity."

9. "Understanding isn't about agreement—it's about respect."

10. "A life of understanding is a life of depth and richness."

11. "Understanding begins with the courage to ask why."

12. "When we understand, we unlock the door to compassion."

13. "The greatest wisdom is found in the pursuit of understanding."

14. "Understanding grows when we open ourselves to new perspectives."

15. "True understanding values people over opinions."

16. "Understanding is the art of seeing the whole picture."

17. "An understanding heart sees beyond the surface."

18. "The path to understanding is paved with patience."

19. "Understanding transforms conflict into opportunity."

20. "To understand another is to honor their truth."

21. "True understanding brings peace to troubled waters."

22. "Seek first to understand, then to be understood."

23. "Understanding grows in the soil of shared stories."

24. "True understanding transcends words and touches the soul."

25. "Understanding unites where ignorance divides."

26. "When we understand ourselves, we begin to understand the world."

27. "Understanding transforms uncertainty into wisdom."

28. "True understanding requires both humility and courage."

29. "An open mind is the doorway to understanding."

30. "Understanding is the bridge between knowledge and wisdom."

31. "The art of understanding begins with letting go of assumptions."

32. "True understanding creates space for healing and connection."

33. "To understand deeply is to love unconditionally."

34. "Understanding builds a foundation for trust."

35. "Every act of understanding strengthens the bonds of humanity."

36. "The essence of understanding is found in its quiet strength."

37. "True understanding listens not just to words but to feelings."

38. "Understanding transforms differences into opportunities for growth."

39. "A life rich in understanding is a life rich in meaning."

40. "The gift of understanding is one we give ourselves and others."

- PART IX -

Purpose, Meaning, and Legacy

Purpose provides life direction; meaning offers depth; legacy guarantees that our efforts last. This part asks you to consider what really counts—that is, to match your behavior with your ideals and design a life that makes a difference.

Every quotation asks you to live deliberately, find meaning in your work, and create a legacy that motivates and cheers on others. Let these words serve as a reminder that your life is a gift and that your mission is the special mark you will leave on the planet at the end of your life.

PURPOSE

1. "Purpose gives direction to the journey of life."

2. "When you find your purpose, you unlock your potential."

3. "Purpose isn't found—it's created through meaningful action."

4. "A life without purpose is like a ship without a compass."

5. "Purpose fuels the heart and guides the mind."

6. "True purpose is rooted in serving something greater than yourself."

7. "The beauty of purpose is that it evolves as you grow."

8. "Purpose turns ordinary days into extraordinary ones."

9. "Discovering your purpose is the beginning of true fulfillment."

10. "Purpose gives meaning to struggles and value to victories."

11. "Your purpose is the gift you give to the world."

12. "Living with purpose transforms existence into experience."

13. "Purpose is the bridge between dreams and reality."

14. "A clear purpose turns challenges into stepping stones."

15. "Purpose aligns your actions with your values."

16. "When you live with purpose, every moment matters."

17. "Purpose is the compass that keeps you on your true path."

18. "Your purpose is unique; it's your personal contribution to the world."

19. "Purpose thrives when passion meets perseverance."

20. "Find your purpose, and you'll find your power."

21. "Purpose is the fire that keeps your spirit alive."

22. "True purpose connects your heart to the needs of the world."

23. "Living with purpose means saying yes to what matters and no to what doesn't."

24. "Purpose transforms work into meaningful service."

25. "A life of purpose leaves no room for regret."

26. "Purpose isn't static; it grows as you do."

27. "Your purpose is the story only you can write."

28. "Purpose gives you the courage to face life's uncertainties."

29. "To live with purpose is to live with clarity and intention."

30. "Purpose is the thread that ties your life's experiences together."

31. "A purposeful life is one lived in alignment with your values."

32. "Purpose gives you the strength to rise above adversity."

33. "When your purpose is clear, your path becomes brighter."

34. "Living with purpose is the ultimate act of self-love."

35. "Purpose is the light that guides you through the storms of doubt."

MEANING

1. "Meaning isn't found in things—it's created in moments."

2. "The search for meaning is the essence of being human."

3. "Life gains meaning when we choose to live intentionally."

4. "Meaning is the thread that connects the past, present, and future."

5. "True meaning comes from the relationships we build."

6. "The smallest acts of kindness add meaning to our lives."

7. "Meaning is the soul's response to the heart's questions."

8. "To find meaning is to discover your place in the world."

9. "Every experience holds the potential for meaning—if you look for it."

10. "Meaning transforms the ordinary into the extraordinary."

11. "Your life's meaning is shaped by the stories you tell yourself."

12. "Meaning grows when you align your actions with your values."

13. "In the pursuit of meaning, we find our deepest truths."

14. "Meaning isn't given; it's uncovered through reflection and growth."

15. "True meaning is rooted in the connections we share with others."

16. "To live with meaning is to live with purpose and passion."

17. "Meaning emerges when you embrace both joy and struggle."

18. "The beauty of meaning is that it evolves as we do."

19. "Life's challenges often reveal its greatest meanings."

20. "Meaning is the lens through which we see life's value."

21. "True meaning is found in the things money cannot buy."

22. "Your life's meaning is the legacy you leave in the hearts of others."

23. "Meaning transforms suffering into strength and loss into love."

24. "The pursuit of meaning is the pursuit of understanding."

25. "Meaning lights the way through life's uncertainties."

26. "In every moment, there's an opportunity to create meaning."

27. "The search for meaning gives depth to life's journey."

28. "When you create meaning, you create a life worth living."

29. "Meaning doesn't come from what you have but from what you give."

30. "To live meaningfully is to live fully."

31. "Meaning adds color to the black-and-white moments of life."

32. "True meaning is found in the courage to be authentic."

33. "Life's greatest meaning is found in the love we share."

34. "The search for meaning connects us to something greater than ourselves."

35. "Meaning is the music of life; it gives rhythm to our days."

LEGACY

1. "Legacy is the story you write with your life."

2. "True legacy is not in possessions but in the lives you touch."

3. "A meaningful legacy begins with purposeful actions."

4. "Your legacy is the echo of your values in the world."

5. "Legacy is built in the moments when no one is watching."

6. "The seeds of your legacy are planted in your daily choices."

7. "Your legacy is the love you leave behind."

8. "A true legacy inspires others to dream and achieve."

9. "Legacy isn't measured in years but in impact."

10. "The greatest legacies are those rooted in kindness and courage."

11. "Your legacy is the light you leave in the hearts of others."

12. "To leave a legacy is to live with intention and purpose."

13. "A lasting legacy is one that uplifts future generations."

14. "Legacy is the bridge between the past and the future."

15. "Your legacy is shaped by the values you choose to live by."

16. "True legacy is the mark of a life well-lived."

17. "The foundation of legacy is built on acts of love and service."

18. "A meaningful legacy is one that sparks change in the world."

19. "Legacy is the story others tell about your life."

20. "Your legacy is the gift you leave for those who follow."

21. "Every small act of kindness contributes to your legacy."

22. "Legacy isn't about being remembered; it's about making a difference."

23. "The beauty of legacy is that it lives on through others."

24. "Your legacy is the reflection of your truest self."

25. "Legacy is written not with words but with deeds."

26. "The best legacies inspire others to believe in their own potential."

27. "A legacy of love is the greatest inheritance you can leave."

28. "Your legacy begins with the choices you make today."

29. "Legacy is the imprint of your life on the hearts of others."

30. "A meaningful legacy transforms the lives it touches."

31. "Legacy is proof that a single life can change the world."

32. "True legacy is found in the joy you bring to others."

33. "Your legacy is the culmination of your values in action."

34. "Legacy is the ripple effect of a purposeful life."

35. "A great legacy is one that inspires hope and courage."

36. "Legacy isn't a destination—it's the footprints you leave behind."

37. "Your legacy is the sum of the love you gave away."

38. "The greatest legacy is a life lived with authenticity and care."

39. "A legacy of service leaves a world richer than you found it."

40. "Legacy is the lasting impact of a heart full of purpose."

- PART X -

Innovation, Creativity, and Progress

Innovation drives change, creativity fuels transfor-mation, and progress is the reward for perseverance. This final part celebrates the power of imagination and the pursuit of excellence. The quotes here encourage you to think outside the box, embrace your creative potential, and strive for continuous improvement.

Innovation begins with a spark, creativity turns ideas into reality, and progress moves us toward a brighter future. Let these words inspire you to innovate boldly, create fearlessly, and push the boundaries of what's possible.

INNOVATION

1. "Innovation begins where imagination meets determination."

2. "The heart of innovation is the courage to think differently."

3. "Innovation turns obstacles into opportunities for greatness."

4. "Every great innovation starts with a single bold idea."

5. "Innovation is the art of finding solutions in the impossible."

6. "The best innovations emerge from asking the right questions."

7. "True innovation is creating what the world doesn't yet know it needs."

8. "Innovation thrives in environments where failure is a step toward success."

9. "An innovative mind sees possibility where others see limits."

10. "Innovation is the bridge between challenges and breakthroughs."

11. "To innovate is to believe that better is always possible."

12. "The spark of innovation can light up the world."

13. "Innovation isn't about perfection; it's about progress."

14. "The most transformative innovations solve problems with simplicity."

15. "Innovation happens when curiosity leads, and fear takes a backseat."

16. "Every innovation begins with a question that challenges the norm."

17. "Innovation doesn't follow the rules—it rewrites them."

18. "To innovate is to dance with uncertainty and lead with creativity."

19. "Innovation asks: What if? Let's try."

20. "The future belongs to those who dare to innovate today."

21. "Innovation isn't just about technology—it's about transformation."

22. "Innovation is the child of curiosity and the parent of progress."

23. "Every innovation starts with someone daring to think bigger."

24. "Innovation is the key that unlocks the door to the future."

25. "True innovation happens at the edge of what's known."

26. "Innovation requires the bravery to fail and the resilience to try again."

27. "The boldest innovations come from the simplest ideas."

28. "To innovate is to see the world not as it is, but as it could be."

29. "Innovation doesn't wait for permission—it forges its own path."

30. "Every act of innovation begins with a leap of faith."

31. "Innovation breathes life into stagnant systems."

32. "The essence of innovation is reimagining the ordinary as extraordinary."

33. "Innovation is fueled by curiosity and driven by purpose."

34. "The most powerful innovations solve problems no one else has noticed."

35. "Innovation transforms the impossible into the inevitable."

CREATIVITY

1. "Creativity is the soul's way of speaking to the world."

2. "Every act of creativity is a step toward self-discovery."

3. "Creativity thrives when we dare to color outside the lines."

4. "True creativity turns chaos into beauty."

5. "The canvas of creativity has no limits—paint freely."

6. "Creativity is not a skill; it's a way of seeing the world."

7. "When creativity flows, possibilities unfold."

8. "The beauty of creativity is found in its infinite expressions."

9. "Creativity is the courage to bring your imagination to life."

10. "Every problem holds the seed of a creative solution."

11. "Creativity transforms the mundane into the magical."

12. "Your creativity is a gift—share it boldly."

13. "The heart of creativity is the willingness to experiment."

14. "Creativity connects the dots in ways no one else can see."

15. "True creativity challenges the status quo and inspires change."

16. "Creativity begins with the question, '*What if?*'"

17. "Every creative act leaves the world a little brighter."

18. "The spark of creativity lights up the darkest corners."

19. "Creativity doesn't follow rules; it creates them."

20. "A creative mind sees potential where others see problems."

21. "Creativity isn't about being perfect; it's about being authentic."

22. "The beauty of creativity lies in its unpredictability."

23. "Creativity is the voice of your imagination calling to be heard."

24. "When creativity and passion meet, extraordinary things happen."

25. "Creativity blooms when we embrace curiosity over certainty."

26. "To create is to bring your unique vision to life."

27. "Creativity is a bridge between your heart and the world."

28. "The most creative solutions often come from the simplest ideas."

29. "Creativity is a journey, not a destination."

30. "Every act of creativity is an act of bravery."

31. "Creativity flourishes in the space between chaos and order."

32. "Your creativity has the power to inspire and transform."

33. "True creativity sees potential in every blank canvas."

34. "Creativity thrives when we stop fearing mistakes."

35. "The essence of creativity is daring to try something new."

PROGRESS

1. "Progress begins with the decision to move forward."

2. "True progress isn't measured in speed but in direction."

3. "Every step, no matter how small, contributes to progress."

4. "Progress is the art of turning effort into excellence."

5. "Progress doesn't happen overnight—it's built one moment at a time."

6. "To progress is to embrace change with courage."

7. "Progress is the reward for persistence and resilience."

8. "The beauty of progress is found in its continuous journey."

9. "Progress asks, '*What's next?*' and answers with action."

10. "True progress values growth over perfection."

11. "Progress happens when effort meets opportunity."

12. "To progress is to challenge the limits of what's possible."

13. "Progress is fueled by hope and driven by determination."

14. "In every failure lies the seed of progress."

15. "Progress doesn't require perfection; it requires persistence."

16. "True progress honors the past while building the future."

17. "The road to progress is paved with intention and effort."

18. "Every small victory is a step forward in progress."

19. "Progress happens when we choose growth over comfort."

20. "To progress is to learn, adapt, and thrive."

21. "The heartbeat of progress is consistent effort."

22. "Progress turns challenges into stepping stones for success."

23. "Every step forward is progress, no matter how small."

24. "True progress is moving closer to your purpose."

25. "The essence of progress is found in its unrelenting pursuit."

26. "Progress isn't linear; it's a dance of steps forward and back."

27. "Progress transforms obstacles into opportunities for growth."

28. "In the rhythm of life, progress is the melody of growth."

29. "Progress is the quiet force that turns dreams into reality."

30. "True progress balances ambition with gratitude."

31. "Progress requires leaving behind what no longer serves you."

32. "Progress is a marathon, not a sprint—pace yourself."

33. "Every act of progress builds momentum for the next step."

34. "The journey of progress begins with a single step."

35. "Progress is fueled by vision and sustained by effort."

36. "True progress celebrates the journey, not just the destination."

37. "Progress transforms potential into reality."

38. "Every step in progress is a vote for your future self."

39. "Progress isn't a destination—it's a mindset of growth."

40. "The essence of progress is turning intention into action."